MW00896407

Darknet: A Beginner's Guide to Staying Anonymous Online

Lance Henderson

Table of Contents

Friend,

My name is Lance and I am the author of this book on encryption security and anonymity. I have been an encryption enthusiast as well as writing about security in general for over a decade. I have been a member of many security and encryption forums since the 1990s, and have been involved with computer technology since the 1980s. If there is a security or encryption program out there, I have used it and experienced its strengths and its shortcomings. I was there when PGP first arrived on the scene, and when Napster was the dominant method of p2p trading. I have used most versions of PGP, Drivecrypt, Bestcrypt, Truecrypt, Tor, Freenet, I2P and every derivative thereof for many years. Today we are constantly bombarded with news by the media of those trawled, raided, arrested, imprisoned, tortured and humiliated because they weren't necessarily breaking any law, but because they did not know the difference between privacy and anonymity. I had been meaning to put together some of the rudimentary elements of encryption security in such a way that a person without any knowledge of security encryption or anonymity could become familiar. It is not a particularly advanced book, but rather a portal from which a beginner can step through with the assurance of anonymity when he is online. To that end I present a few tools (mostly free) at your disposal to accomplish this lofty goal. If you're an advanced user, you just might learn some hidden vulnerabilities in your favorite anonymity program.

A PhD in computer science is not required to use encryption. Neither are you required to be a programmer of any sort. You only have to know your way around your operating system and be able to follow directions to the letter. If you know how to install an operating system, or for that matter, any application at all, then you can safely use encryption programs to preserve your own digital data and safety.

"If you want total security, go to prison. There you're fed, clothed, given medical care and so on. The only thing lacking ... is freedom"

- Dwight Eisenhower

Chapter 1 - Privacy and Anonymity

If you're like one of the many billions of people on the planet who use the internet to surf the net, check email, download programs or do any kind of online work, then you probably know there are risks associated with being a habitual internet user. It is not your fault that there are so many latent traps and pitfalls associated with online spelunking, in whatever form that may be. It is just a fact of life that the Good lives alongside the Evil in our lives, offline or online. This book is meant as a beginner's guide to distinguish between the Good and the Evil, and to conceal your online footprint. To be a ghost on the internet, that is our aim. This book is not necessarily for the advanced, such as those who teach computer science courses, but rather it is for those who would like to learn to surf without compromising their identity, or having their online habits tracked 24/7, and who engage in some risky speech against their government once in a blue moon. It is also for those who might not know about some of the little known vulnerabilities in their favorite "anonymous" software programs. In the end, you just might learn there is a vast difference between "anonymity" and "privacy".

Let's start with the basics. I'll just put this out there so you know the weight of the privacy situation entirely. As of 2014, you are always being tracked on the internet in just about every way you can imagine. Search engines, cookie managers, download managers and everything you do online has the potential to make someone, somewhere, a LOT of money. Most of the time, this is because laser-targeted advertising is extremely profitable. The more they know about your habits, the more money they make.

How?

Simple. If they know more about your fears, your likes and dislikes, and how and where you spend your money, they can deliver targeted advertising to you. Laser targeted advertising. That means more power for them, less for you. Now, advertising in and of itself is not such a bad thing, but neither is a loaded gun sitting on top of the fridge. By itself it can do nothing. However it is the method of execution that defines its usefulness.

If you type any medical search term into a major search engine such as Google, Yahoo, or Bing, soon enough you'll start to see targeted ads. If you search for "how to cure a hangover", you might not see anything right away, since hangovers generally don't last that long. However if you were to type "how to cure herpes", you will likely be typing variations of that sentence over the course of a few weeks or months since it is not an easy condition to treat. Eventually you would see pay-per-click ads start to manifest themselves in your search engine results in the top corners. These ads might be selling all manner of snake-oil remedies for the cure to herpes, or they might be referrals to medical specialists. The bottom line is this: why do they think you have this disease? The answer is because you repeatedly typed it into the search engine over the course of days/months. Over the course of a year, how much do you reveal about your medical history and identity to your favorite search engine? Do you ever wish you could keep this information private?

They like to "bubble" your identity based on how you search: the time between searches, the time of day, your country, your area. With the help of a very specific item in your internet portfolio called an IP address, they can even find out where you live, who your ISP is, and chart a course right to your very doorstep. With the help of Google Maps, and a whole plethora of other mapping applications, this can potentially lead to some very annoying and/or embarrassing situations. Do you think this information would be valuable to door-to-door salesmen? Or perhaps a company that sends out mailed advertisements? Of course.

But first things first, let's briefly say a word about the difference between privacy and anonymity since many would-be geeks confuse the two. They are not the same thing. Not by a long shot.

Anonymity & Privacy - The Differences

While we shouldn't waste time splitting hairs here, it is probably a good idea to distinguish between the terms "privacy" and "anonymity". The two terms are not really as interchangeable as you think. Let's say that you have Firefox running, and you are working from home with a direct connection to your ISP. You don't want anyone knowing what you're doing, so you select the "private mode" tab in Firefox. This disables cookies and inhibits the ability to store any remembered websites (unless you choose to do so).

However this privacy only goes so far. It does nothing for the IP address problem we discussed earlier. Search engines still see it, as does your internet service provider. Both entities know which sites you visit and for how long, based on your IP address. In short, they can see everything. Your wife can't, however. That is why the privacy mode in web browsers were built: to keep the sites you visit private and out of the public view. Is this privacy enough for your needs? You certainly have some level of privacy, but anonymity is another matter. Anonymity takes privacy to an entirely different level, where the IP address, and thus anything you do online, is extinguished like a wet cloth to a candle's flame through layer after layer of digital barriers. If you want to have privacy, use Firefox's private mode, or use a VPN service provider in conjunction with this feature to ensure no one else in your household can see your online footprints. This assumes that they do not have access to your laptop or PC. If that's the case, it's game over.

If on the other hand you want anonymity, there are several tools are your disposal, one of which is to use the Tor network. In doing so, you will guarantee yourself strict anonymity and be assured of simple privacy as well...provided you don't do something stupid like blurt out enough info (on a forum, for instance) that narrows you down to a city or state.

"If money is your hope for independence you will never have it. The only real security that a man will have in this world is a reserve of knowledge, experience, and ability."

Henry Ford

Chapter 2 - The Anonymous Tor Network

Every Internet Service Provider assigns an IP address to every user who logs into their network. From there, you can connect to the millions of websites, newsgroups, and online applications that you enjoy most. IP addresses are like phone numbers. They tell your computer where to connect and send packets of data. They need this information to not only send data, such as html code, but also flash code so you can watch Youtube videos. These are targeted with ads, too. And if you bring up task manager in Windows, you can see Flash player running. Do you think Adobe is not sending data back to them about your habits? Let's continue.

So, if the security of online privacy involves concealing the IP address between two computers, how do those two computers talk to each other without a direct connection? If you hide the phone number, how do you make the call? The answer is simple: you have someone else in another country dial the number for you. This is the first step to being anonymous online. Do not use the IP address (yours) as a direct connection. Hire a middle man to do the talking for you. How is this possible? There are several ways. You can use the free online program called <u>Tor</u>, which acts a relay point between you and your online destination. There are also paid services called VPNs (virtual private networks) as well as other anonymous networks like Freenet and I2P, but we'll get into the specifics of those later.

First and foremost, let's talk about Tor. It is the quintessential solution to online privacy, since it masks your IP address. The websites you connect to have no way of knowing where you live, which ISP you are using, or what your browsing habits are. When you connect to the Tor network, you are establishing a conduit whereby if you connect to a website (Google for instance), it connects through several layers of IP addresses, or "onion layers" to reach its destination. You send out a message, email, or some type of communication. The message then goes to Bob, Jane and Herb, then finally reaches the end of the line…your favorite webpage. It routes data (backwards/forwards) through an onion later of IP addresses, so that no one adversary can see who sent what without very significant resources.

As you have probably guessed, there is a small speed hit in doing this. In order to hide your IP address, several "hops" or intermediaries, have to be jumped through. Like portals. Without going into too much technical detail, let's just say that these hops serve a very valuable purpose: to keep your private communications out of the hands of those that intend to snoop on you. Since your IP address changes every time you login to the Tor network, they can't "bubble" you effectively and target you with ads because you look like a different person from a foreign country to them each time you login. The Tor relay will end up giving you a different country to "pop-out" from with each session of your Tor browser, thus making it impossible to know your origin or where you will go next.

Let's examine an analogy between Tor and regular internet usage. You're sitting in your living room browsing anonymously via the Tor network. Your wife on the other hand is sitting in the kitchen on her Macbook, browsing without Tor. You might wonder if her browsing habits break your own anonymity. They don't...up to a point. While your isp doesn't know what *you* are doing online, they certainly do in regards to your wife.

Imagine yourself driving down Main Street in a Mercedes with tinted windows. No one can peer inside to see what you are doing at the stoplight. Not even the cops. Your wife on the other hand has non-tinted windows. People can glance over without any effort and tell if she is smoking a cigarette, listening to her iPod or talking on her phone. You are anonymous. She is not. The ISP along with any websites she visits can see everything she does online. They can't see what you are doing, however.

Firefox (and many other browsers) talk to different hosts, with the router acting as the traffic cop. An example:

Your machine: Port X, Machine A (Tor: all encrypted traffic)
Your wife: Port Y, Machine B (without Tor: all visible traffic)

It's like shooting fish in a barrel, and for the NSA, even easier than that. This same concept also applies with other things you may do on your machine while using Tor. If you use BitTorrent, your ISP can still see what you do on the P2P network even if you are running Tor simultaneously. But it cannot see the contents of the Tor network.

Thus, don't do anything on your P2P network that you wouldn't want your ISP to know about. Tor however is a different story since they cannot see what is going on between Tor relays. For all intents and purposes, Tor is like a cloak of invisibility that shields you from the sight of all onlookers, unless you have accidentally ripped a hole in the cloak (i.e. turned on javascript). If you are thinking, "Wow, it might be cool to run BitTorrent through Tor so I won't get sued". A nice goal, except BitTorrent devs aren't falling over themselves to implement this feature with Tor, and the Tor network can't really handle the bandwidth anyway. You'll just make everyone else miserable by downloading those 720p Blu-Ray rips you can easily get from Usent (and with SSL, you're not likely to get sued.)

It might be prudent to spell out some of the best practices of using the Tor network should you decide to use it. First, although the Tor package comes with a preconfigured Firefox browser, there are still some rules you should follow that might not be apparent.

1.)   Never give any compromising information on the Tor network that could be used to identify you. This means using your credit card for purchases, accessing your bank account, or logging into a social media site like Facebook. Card transaction are traceable. Tor, in fact, may even result in flagging transactions done via a tor exit node.

2.)   Never mix browsers. Don't use the same browser you browse every day to Facebook and your ISP email as you do to access the Tor network. Super cookies can give away which sites you visit outside of Tor and can lead to a correlation attack on your identity/IP address.

3.)   Always disable javascript. The reason for this is that exploits can be utilized to reveal your IP address through using flash. Flash videos such as those on Youtube only work if this is enabled. After installation of Tor, ensure that the settings in the NoScript plugin are ON and not off by default in the plugins options screen.

4.)   Install a bare minimum of browser plugins. You want to be as vanilla as everyone else. Too many addins, plugins, games, etc., can act as an identity beacon--fonts you use, time of day you use certain features, can all be used to build a profile on you. BE VANILLA.

5.)   Disable any automatic updates in the browser's options tab. This also includes updates for any addons. You should update manually, not automatically.

Chapter 3 - Tor and Torrents

A word about torrents and the Tor network. It might seem on the surface that running your torrent client through the Tor network would be an obviously beneficial idea. After all, if Tor can cloak your regular Firefox downloads, surely it can do the same with torrents too, right? Well, yes and no. Yes, you could route your traffic through Tor using your favorite torrent client, however this is not a good idea for several reasons. The first is that Tor was never developed to withstand the kind of punishing traffic bandwidth that usually comes from torrenting.

Secondly, most torrent clients like uTorrent, BitSpirit, and libTorrent are not coded properly to make you anonymous on the Tor network. They often will ignore their socks proxy settings since UDP protocol is heavily involved with torrenting, and will send your real IP address to the tracker, thereby defeating the purpose of using Tor completely. Tor in fact still does what it is coded to do: send whatever packets anonymously through the Tor network to your destination. However, it sends your IP address within the torrent tracker right along with it...anonymously.

It would be like sending a secret message in an envelope directly to the person you are attempting to hide that message from. This is not a problem with the Tor application, but rather the way torrent trackers are coded. The only fix would be if the torrent application coders themselves rewrote their applications to work harmoniously with the Tor network, something they probably will not get around to doing anytime soon (and much to the glee of Tor developers).

Tor Onion Sites

One of the most secretive elements of the Tor network is the existence of Tor Onion websites, which are pseudo top level domains acting as anonymous hidden services. In other words, they are hidden in that they can only be accessed by the Tor users themselves residing within the Tor network, rather from the open web. The motive for the creation of such hidden sites is so that the admin of the site as well as those accessing such sites cannot be traced. Since onion sites that are based on the hidden service protocol cannot be accessed from the regular internet, the address of the onion site you are looking for must be known. You can connect to an onion website on Tor just as you can a regular website, by typing the address into the address bar. For example, you might want to go to Tor2Web, in which case the address is:

http://tor2web.org/.

A warning about tor2web: it is intended to offer one-sided security, that is, to protect the identity of those publishing content on Tor, not those browsing it. If you want to be secure while browsing you'll need to install the Tor application. Convenience and speed should always take a back seat where security is concerned.

Needless to say, a hidden network would not stay completely benign of nefarious webmasters if it wasn't indeed anonymous. To that end, the Hidden Wiki was developed, a singular .onion page with a wikipedia-like structure outlining in explicit detail everything from political activists to every conceivable criminal group imaginable. There are links to hundreds of various .onion sites dealing with everything from how to obtain illegal drugs, warez operations, virus creation, anonymous use of Bitcoins, illegal pornography, hacked Paypal accounts and even how to hire contract killers. Needless to say, some of these sites need to be taken with a grain of salt.

Be aware of your own country's laws regarding what can legally be obtained. What goes around in Amsterdam or Japan may not fly straight with the authorities in the USA. Remember that information that exists in Deep Web is just that: information. By itself, the information can do nothing. Words are just rearranged letters to get your point across. Pictures and videos are simply ones and zeros moving across your display. It is what they are eventually used for that define their ethics.

At the core of it, the Hidden Wiki is not terribly dissimilar from any run-of-the-mill black market operation offline. It just so happens to be online, and accessible by anyone with a little search engine sleuthing capability. Not all of the information in the Deep Web is used for nefarious purposes. Like Freenet, there are a lot of different sites that concentrate on exposing human rights abuse, political corruption, and government scandals involving high-level politicians. In the end, it is what you do with the data that determines the criminal element.

Testing your IP address visibility on Tor

When you have installed Tor, you may want to test your IP address to see if it really is broadcasting your Tor IP and not your real IP address. If you installed the default package of Tor, then Tor will show you the IP you are broadcasting as your start page. If you want to check it yourself, then go to

http://whatismyipaddress.com/.

This will show you not only your IP address, but your internet service provider as well, and where it is located on google maps. It will also show city and country. When you are using Tor, you will see a different city/country than the one you currently reside in. Mark down what your IP address is outside of Tor, and check this site when your launch Tor if you're especially paranoid (I am).

VPNs

The last few years have seen an emergence of many different VPN (virtual private network) providers with server farms in just about every country. What a VPN does is somewhat similar to what the Tor network does. It sends a different IP address to your destination, whether that is a webpage, usenet provider, or webhost. There are some pros and cons to this. First, it is not free. A VPN will cost the same amount you would get for Usenet service: about ten dollars per month. This amount fluctuates from provider to provider. Sometimes it is a little more, sometimes a bit less, but all providers have you login to their service the same way you would an ISP. Most of the configuration is automatic and doesn't require any technical wizardry to setup. Five minutes, give or take.

Another major difference is that while Tor provides anonymity, and is free, a VPN will provide you with *privacy*, but not necessarily *anonymity*. This is because the middle man, the VPN in this case, knows your real IP address. They have to know this information in order to forward your requests. The VPN service is built upon a different technology than Tor. It is built for *speed* and *stability*. Torrenting, you say? Knock yourself out.

Further, let's say that you're a Chinese dissident. You don't like the way your country is headed in regards to free speech and human rights. You can't exactly criticize the Chinese government in the Saturday paper can you? Of course not. So what is a good, law-abiding dissident to do? You build a news website using a VPN in another country and relay your dissent through that internet portal. You don't necessarily have to build a website. You could simply setup your newsreader to access Usenet via the VPN connection. In that way, the Chinese government could not determine the origin of any anti-governmental messages through the use of the IP address (unless of course you hint of incriminating personal information that narrows down your location).

You can also access forbidden places by the Chinese government, such as Facebook, Skype, private chat rooms and even Usenet. The reason these kinds of places are blocked by the Great Firewall of China is precisely because they are fertile ground for free speech enthusiasts. While this may sound like an easy way to circumvent the Chinese police, remember that most VPN providers offer connections through almost every civilized country you can think of. If you are a Chinese dissident, I wouldn't connect to a VPN located in China, but rather Canada or perhaps a country hostile to China. Most VPN providers offer a selection of many servers to choose from in which to route your messages and traffic.

On that note, let's talk a bit about law enforcement and VPNs. Many in the past have erroneously thought that a VPN carried with it a strong dose of anonymity, similar to what Tor offered. It doesn't quite stack up that way. A VPN service offers privacy, not anonymity, as we stated. They do not route your data through intermediaries the way Tor does. Depending on which VPN you choose, you could end up with one in Switzerland who will not cave to anyone's request for subscriber information outside of Sweden. On the other hand, you might have a US based provider who will bow down to the whims of any judge's warrant for subscriber information in a New York minute.

While most are perfectly safe for purposes of torrents and the like, one should think twice about using a VPN in a western country for felonious offenses, as they will most likely give your name and address up to law enforcement in order to stave off any fines and/or trouble by the government. There are of course ways around this, such as not using your credit card and paying anonymously, however sometimes it is better not to use a VPN at all for those kinds of purposes (think hackers, smuggling, illicit banned goods, drugs etc). Vpns have never been built with anonymity in mind. Tread carefully.

"If you go to a coffee shop or at the airport, and you're using open wireless, I would use a VPN service that you could subscribe for 10 bucks a month. Everything is encrypted in an encryption tunnel, so a hacker cannot tamper with your connection."

Kevin Mitnick

Chapter 4: Tor Relays

"Who can you trust? Nobody, cause nobody wants you here."

Those words, uttered by Sean Connery in The Untouchables, are as appropriate for darknet discussions as they are for the mafia. But let's be realistic for a moment. There are, as you read this, ten thousand more organized crime syndicates spread out over the net than you will ever come across in the "Deep Web". They run the same secure, enterprise-grade software that Wall Street banks use and cloak themselves better than Ringwraiths. No outside eyes peer in unless the alphabet agency has a guy on the inside. Cartels like these rake in millions in drugs, arms, counterfeit pharmaceuticals, mercs and excel at human trafficking. Yes, even child slaves, as well as child porn.

The Deep Web is similar, but not that similar. But those who are for outlawing it completely are really advocating for more control rather than for less crime, as was the case with Prohibition. They claim the negatives outweigh the positives. Let's say a guy in North Korea gets curious as to why his government is censoring information from him. He wants to know why. So he uses Tor to access websites blocked by the North Korean regime

(Facebook for instance, to hook up with an uncle who may have escaped to S. Korea). And he does so anonymously. So that is one positive trait.

But this, they say, does not outweigh the child porn, contract killers and heroin runners. They say, people aren't going to Tor to discuss ways of avoiding the mine fields on the border and neither are they discussing the latest enlightenment from Tibet. Yes, anonymity has its meritorious moments, but someone who wants to hide almost always does so at the circumvention of the law. There are only so many North Koreans, after all.

They assume, quite wrongly, that those criminals engaged in the above activities would cease to exist. They are wrong. These were around before Tor and the Deep Web were even a spark in the developer's minds, and will thrive regardless of what government regulations are cooked up by congress critters. The same as it was during Prohibition.

Hazards of running a Tor Exit Node

In 2012, an Austrian named William Weber, an IT admin, was arrested for running Tor servers that route anonymous traffic over the Tor network. The charge? Distributing illegal images. Police detected the data coming off one of the nodes he ran. A police raid ensued. Searched his home. Confiscated his Xbox, iPods, all drives and miscellaneous electronics and even his legally owned firearms. The court order revealed one of the Tor exit nodes (he ran seven) was transporting the data.

Notice, we did not state that *he* transported the data. The data in question is going to come down on some node, be it his or someone else's. That is how Tor works: via encrypted traffic that gets piped through servers on its own IP address, through various layers (hence the term Onion layer) and decrypted back into its initial form. An ISP cannot discern the contents in transit. However, law enforcement can see the contents coming out of a node that was sent from the other side of the globe. Holding a Tor node operator responsible would be like holding a forum administrator responsible because some anonymous poster said he was going to kill the president.

Misuse of Tor end nodes are fairly common. Back in 2008, a man was arrested by German police after bomb threats passed through his Tor node, and similarly, they confiscated all electronics--hardware, software, and threatened imprisonment because someone abused his generosity. These kinds of cases bring up a few parallels. Should the Austrian government sue Google for having illegal data flowing through its servers? We're not only talking about images or bomb threats. Warez, kidnapping, extortion, bribery, espionage, a long laundry list of crimes occur on a daily basis via their search engine, and though Google cooperates with law enforcement (as Weber did), when was the last time you heard Google's servers confiscated by a court order?

And then there is encryption. Should Drivecrypt and Truecrypt developers be held liable for helping illegal enterprises? Truecrypt is a software used quite heavily by Mexican cartels as well as organized crime in the United States. Law enforcement, particularly the FBI, tends to shoot first and ask questions later. Maybe. If they're in a good mood (or ordered to by a judge). Meanwhile, your electronics are confiscated and your reputation damaged.

The entire ordeal has been setting dangerous precedent for years, as any average Joe who just happens to pass some part of an illegal data packet through his connection (or unsecured WiFi) can be prosecuted. Furthermore, police are not known for their technical aptitude, in Austria or anywhere else. They took his Xbox360 and anything else plugged in that looked about as complex as a toaster. We mustn't allow Tor node operators to be scapegoats. If Tor dies, innocent people die. They won't get the word out about corrupt government actions without risking their own lives. And they shouldn't *have* to risk anything to get the word out.

As of 2014, no one has been sued or prosecuted in a U.S. court of law for running a Tor relay (unlike those using BitTorrent). Furthermore, using Tor as well as running a Tor relay is perfectly legal under U.S. law.

Benefits of Running a Tor Exit Node:

We've talked a little about the risks of being a Tor exit mode. You might be saying, well, the risks far outweigh the benefits. And in some places, you're right. But it depends on where you live, the laws, the bandwidth, your setup, etc.
So what are the benefits?

- Help people all over the world browse the net anonymously (esp. censorship-prone countries)
- Provide support for the network
- Exit nodes are always scarce. Your generosity supports development.
- Defeat tyranny (what's that? Well, North Korea for one)
- Prevent websites/search engines from tracking you
- Help others get beyond the Great Firewall of China
- Join the Rebel Alliance (yeah right, you're thinking...)

At this point it might be prudent to relay my own experience. The first time I used Tor, I was already fairly good as not only admin of several websites and hosted machines, but quite good at encryption. My frame of thought was, if I was no slouch at encryption, Tor would be a piece of cake.

And it was...for a while. I had plenty of bandwidth available, so I jumped right in.

Being in North America at the time, it would be a few weeks to get up to speed on all the pros and cons of Tor relays, and not from the technical standpoint, but the legal. I envisioned Blackhawk helicopters and car chases involving white vans with license plates that read "NOTOJ" should I be so unlucky to screw up my configuration. Putting my paranoia aside, I finally got it running full speed, and studied the network logs like a hawk to see what it was doing. And I was well-pleased. Full of pride, you might say.

Tor traffic trickled in like a sprinkle before a storm, and after three days my node had spread just as the bandwidth limits I had preset kicked in. The feeling was euphoric. Addicting. I envisioned some tech-starved villager in North Korea accessing something verboten by the Korean government. I kept thinking about Matthew Broderick in WarGames and the famous line, "The only way to win the game, was not to play." Well, I tweaked it to add, "...by the Man's rules." It was all good.

Until a week later when my ISP ordered me to cut the Tor umbilical. It was polite, but stern. It seemed a few complaints sailed their way. As my luck would have it, that North Korean villager turned out to be a swarm of torrentors using Tor to evade the trackers setup by the record industry. It.

hampered Tor's bandwidth like a hurricane had set upon it.

"Torrents?" I said. "Really?"

Yes indeed. And even though I lived in Canada at the time and wasn't worried about a torrent of lawsuits, I still did not want other Tor users to be hindered by greedy users. The problem I ran into was that filtering torrent traffic is a bit counterproductive since BitTorrent is able to run on any standard port. I tried blocking ports 80 and 443 (web traffic). It wasn't a silver bullet, however, since torrent users could still use other ports. BitTorrent clients like uTorrent and BitLord can run on any port, almost all randomly chosen. Thus every port you add to your exit node can connect to another client listening on that same port. Some users even enable a range of ports, thereby increasing the chance of getting a DMCA takedown for you.

Hence, we come to the Reduced Exit Policy of Tor, an alternative to the default exit policy. You are still able to connect and at the same time block TCP ports (usually) used by BitTorrent users. Below are a couple of port lists to check against BitTorrent clients:

https://secure.wikimedia.org/wikipedia/en/wiki/List_of_TCP_and_UDP_port_numbers

http://www.speedguide.net/ports.php

What should become clear as crystal at this point is that you should not run an exit relay from your house, with emphasis on *should not*. Why not? Because of the aforementioned scenarios with law enforcement. As we've seen in prior cases, it is quite easy for them to get a judge's signature (a judge who knows squat about Tor) on a no-knock warrant in the USA should they start sniffing your traffic. Not only will they take your computer, but everything with connectivity, which these days includes TVs and monitors. Much better to run the exit relay from a commercial provider (and there are many). A few in the U.S. who are not only knowledgeable about Tor, but have the support needed to deal with abuse cases are as follows:

    Amazon Web Services (AWS)
    AmeriNOC
    Arvixe
    Axigy
    ChunkHost
    Team Cinipac
    Cyberonic
    Ethr.net
    Evolucix
    Future Hosting

A full comprehensive list is available at the Tor Wiki that covers many countries, each with their own subset of laws dealing with anonymity services (and extensive comments on each). In the event you do decide to run a Tor relay from home however, make sure you inform your ISP and ascertain whether you have their full support (i.e. no surprises a month down the line). The abuse complaints will come sooner or later, just as they did for me. The Tor forums have a list of ISPs that are friendly towards Tor and are knowledgeable about the network, in addition to ones that are not.

Chapter 5 - Freenet

Freenet is unlike any other anonymizing beast on the entire internet. It takes quite a wizardly mind to crack its protection and to that, it is a bit like chess: easy to grasp the basics, long and difficult to become a master. Built in 2000, Freenet is a vast, encrypted datastore spanning thousands of connected computers across the globe, all distributing encrypted contents from one computer to another. To this end, it is somewhat similar to a P2P program like Emule. Except with eEule, every file, whether it mp3, rar or iso is out there in the open for weeks, months and years, along with the IP addresses, trumpeting who downloaded and uploaded every file. You know what you upload, and what you download, and so does everyone else.

Freenet is different in this regard. While your IP address is visible, what you are uploading out of your datastore is not. You initially setup the size of the datastore for others to download from you. This datastore is encrypted. You have no idea what will eventually be inside, as the contents are encrypted. It is a bit like a postal worker delivering the mail. He has no idea what is in the package he is delivering. That is not his job. His job is to deliver the contents to its destination. Therein is the strength of Freenet. While you can see your downloads merrily trickle their way down to your laptop, there is no way to decrypt your datastore's content and see what it is you're passing along to the nearest node. And to that, the bigger the datastore, the more efficiently Freenet runs. After one inserts a file into Freenet, the user is free to shutdown their pc. This is unlike torrents in that the stability of the torrent file is dependent on the length of online seeds. Thus, high reliability is a factor with Freenet files, as the file is spread between encrypted blocks residing in the Freenet system.

Freenet is slow. So slow in fact, that you may not see any measurable progress in download speed for a couple hours or so after install, and it may be a day before you can see extensive progress with old (unpopular) files. Don't get discouraged because of this. It will speed up gradually over time.

Now, with your IP address out there in the open, you might be tempted to think it is not very anonymous. Nothing could be further from the truth. Whatever you download is encrypted from one end of Freenet to the other, and decrypted on your PC. No one looking in from the outside can see who requested which file or message. No one on the inside knows either, except you. For this reason alone, it is extremely censorship-resistant. This level of anonymity requires each node that requests data to operate in "hops", from many intermediaries, similar to what you would see in Tor.

However, no node knows who requested which file, thus giving a high level of anonymity. This requirement carries a price in that downloads as well as uploads are initially extremely slow, especially for new data inserts.

Let's say you want to share an iso dvd image on this network. You fire up Frost (a front-end addon for Freenet), then hit insert, then select the file. Then depending on how big your file is, you could be waiting for a long time, say several hours, for the file to finish. If this file had been inserted three months prior, and was very popular, with dozens of users trying to fetch said file, then that file would download very fast. However this is not usually the case with new files since every kernel of data on Freenet operates faster if and only if it is a popular file.

There are two types of security protocols that Freenet offers: Darknet and Openet. For Openet, you connect to other users, called "strangers". There is nothing sinister about this, as this is what the Freenet developers envisioned that most beginners would use. The IP address of said strangers is visible, but the anonymity of Freenet isn't nested in the security of the IP address like Tor, but rather it is nested in the encryption methods of the distributed datastore.

The other security option, which you are given at installation, is Darknet, where you will connect to "friends" rather than "strangers". These will be Freenet users that you will have (presumably) previously exchanged node references, which are public security keys. With Darknet mode, it is assumed that you will have a higher level of trust, as your node reference is related to your online Freenet identity. Needless to say, this mode is not to be taken lightly. You really do have to TRUST those you add to this protocol. That is, the darknet protocol.

Within Freenet, there are no censors. Every kind of free speech is allowable and often encouraged. The very way in which Freenet is programmed makes it impossible to remove any message from the system by a censor. Individual users may opt to erase certain comments from the frost system, for instance, but this is only at the local level, on their machine, and not the Freenet network itself. Thus, no religious group for instance can force others in the network to conform to their belief and discussion system. No one on Freenet may deem information so offensive that it must be removed. Not even Freenet developers.

Needless to say, this has some negative consequences in that anyone may say anything to anyone at any time. Some Freesites on the Freenet network are plagued by spammers, identity thieves, terrorists, molesters, government anarchists and software pirates. The Freenet developers have stated this is a necessary evil of sorts in allowing 100% free speech to reign free. It could be argued that one should not allow illicit digital goods to be exchanged between users just so people could speak freely, however one of the stated purposes of Freenet is to preserve such a system in the even of societal collapse or oppression.

While there are no rules to govern Freenet by in the sense of censoring unsightly posts, a few guidelines have been posted in scattered parts of Freenet that should probably be heeded:

1.) Never give anyone on Freenet your node-reference, as this contains information that could be exploited to correlate your Freenet identity with your IP address.

2.) Same rule as Usenet: Don't give in to trolling activity. Trolling by its very nature flourishes with the more responses it receives. Ignore them.

3.) Never give out any personal info: your location, where you grew up, which restaurants you like most, what kinds of clothing stores you shop at, as these could zero-in on your location

4.) Take notice of different regionally spelled words (labor vs. labour, color vs. colour: these could reveal your home country).

5.) Never use any nickname that is the very same unique nickname you use for opennet forums. Use popular nicknames like Shadow, John, Peter and the like.

The highest security setting can be a bit foreboding, but perhaps necessary in countries where criticizing the government could land you a lifetime in a work camp. It has an encrypted password option to encrypt Freenet usage. This setting is in the security configuration, along with a host of other options of varying system requirements. The higher the security setting, the slower Freenet will run as it will use more resources to cover your footsteps.

When first installing Freenet, it will likely take no more than a few minutes, while asking you which security level you would like to operate at (normal up to maximum). After that and a bit of time allowed for Freenet to find nodes to connect to, you'll be presented with a previously hidden world where a Freenet index lists every possible combination of Freesites available. Everything from anarchy sites to Iranian news, to pirated copies of books, films and game roms and even a few political how to documents describing how to protest a corrupt government without getting caught will be indexed. These are the types of things typically either censored by Google in China, or deindexed altogether. The only thing missing is a disclaimer at the bottom of the screen welcoming you to the deepest, darkest depths of the internet, known as Darknet.

Optionally, you may run Freenet from an encrypted Truecrypt container file. You will need to create a Truecrypt volume that is sufficiently large enough to hold whatever files you intend on downloading from Freenet. Remember to keep in mind that when Freenet asks you how large you want the datastore to be, the size you choose could be a benefit to other Freenet users. The larger the datastore, the more efficient the Freenet network operates. That is not to say that downloads will *always* come down faster, but rather encrypted data will last longer on the network. This is similar to the retention times that Usenet providers talk about when they try to sell their servers to you. The higher the data retention, the longer the files on the network will last. There is also another bonus to having a large datastore, say fifty gigabytes or so. Files that you may request may already be in your datastore after having run Freenet for some time, thereby shortening the time to retrieve them.

With your Truecrypt container you can run Freenet with the volume mounted and not worry about your Freenet activities being used against you in case of your computer being confiscated. You can also do the same for your Tor browser as well. Install Tor browser bundle to a mounted Truecrypt container and only run the program when mounted.

Frost

Frost is a separate application than Freenet, which acts as a front-end. It makes browsing on the Freenet network more akin to browsing Usenet newsgroups. Download at:

http://jtcfrost.sourceforge.net

After running Freenet, you can optionally run Frost simultaneously to download inserts from the Freenet network. It is not mandatory but it is incredibly helpful. Run Freenet, then Frost, and then wait an hour or so for Frost to find some groups, and then hit the globe button at the top panel to subscribe to groups. These groups all have discussions going about every topic under the sun. Some of them are fairly dead, with almost no discussion at all, and others swarm with activity.

Frosty Tips:

1.) If you started downloading something in Frost, finish it in Frost
2.) Like Usenet, don't troll the boards. It will get you put on user's "ignore" list and they will henceforth not see any messages from your nick.
3.) Never reveal your node reference to anyone on the Frost boards, as it could be used to locate you.
4.) Set days to download backwards to 60 (or however long you wish). Just be aware that it may

take several days to retrieve all messages if you select a very large amount of days.

5.) In the options/preferences tab, you may adjust the setting to ignore comments from users with less than four messages attached to their nickname. This is very effective at eliminating most spam messages on the board.

Chapter 6 - Truecrypt

It would be folly if we went to all this work of laying out the security options to keep our online footprint out of nefarious hands and not say something about our offline footprint. Put simply, you should tread carefully with your offline habits just as you should your online persona.

Let's say you're in your favorite cafe. You're sipping your ice cappuccino with your laptop in the corner of the coffee scented shop and have to make a break for the restroom. It'll only take a minute or so, right? While you're in there, the guy sitting at the next table decided to insert a USB key into your laptop and upload a keylogger virus into your machine. This keylogger is ridiculously small in size, and can hide undetected by most users. It can even disguise itself as a windows service and look just like any other svchost process, all the while taking snapshots of your screen, recording everything you typed for the remainder of that day, and emailing them to whomever installed the virus. You would be a bit worried if you knew about it.

However, most don't realize they leave themselves vulnerable to such attacks in public places. Some experts have referred to this as the "evil maid attack", after a scenario whereby you are in a hotel and briefly step outside for a moment and at which point the maid comes in and has physical access to your running machine. They now have access to every cookie stored by your browser in addition to any credit card numbers you have used, possible phone numbers/emails of friends, and the like. How to prevent this?

For starters, to prevent identity theft you need to seriously consider full-disk encryption. This is not nearly as complex as you might think. It is ridiculously easy encrypt your boot drive and costs you nothing, and potentially saves you from months of headache.

There are several encryption apps at your disposal: the paid programs, such as PGP, Drivecrypt, and Phonecrypt, and the popular free versions, PGP and Truecrypt. There are a few differences between them but the one thing to take away from both free and paid versions is that they prohibit anyone from booting your computer, laptop, or phone without the password.

Truecrypt is free, and does this by creating a 256 AES encryption key. You install the application, select your drive you want to encrypt, and select your passphrase and create an encrypted key. Simple.

How does this benefit you? Well, the next time that thief who stole your laptop tries to boot up the hard drive, without the password he'll be out of luck. He is presented with this password field before windows even boots, and if it is not keyed in correctly, the drive halts. The password, if sufficiently long, is enough to withstand almost any brute-force attack, even by the NSA. Just make sure to use a passphrase that will be easy to remember, but long enough to thwart any attacker: 15-character passphrase with upper/lowercase letters with a number or two.

Just how strong is Truecrypt? It is considered impossible to crack, on the order of millions of years. It would take quantum computers eons to crack even a moderately length passphrase using brute-force methods. In all likelihood the absolute weakest link is *you.*

Keyloggers can obtain your password if you are unlucky enough to get one. However, these are a fairly rare occurrence if you keep your operating system, anti-virus and anti-malware programs up to date. The other weakest link is your passphrase. You would be surprised at just how many people use their own personal information in their passphrases. Doing this might make the password easier to remember, but also easier to crack. A good passphrase is made up of lower and upper case characters in addition to spaces, which lend more entropy bits to the protection. At each instance a bit is added to a passphrase, the computational crunching requirement to crack such passphrase is doubled. If I were living in North Korea or China, for example, I would seriously consider a passphrase that was at least twenty characters long, with some keyboard symbols thrown in for good measure. Most people do not like to remember a twenty character passphrase however, so they use a less random one.

Drivecrypt is another encryption program, but it is not open-source and is not free. I have used this program for eight years and have to say if money is a concern, then go with Truecrypt as it has many of the same functions that Truecrypt does, and for zero cost. Drivecrypt has an option called "bootauth" which is short for boot authorization. The install process is similar to Truecrypt, though the bootup passphrase screen is a little different. You boot your hard drive, and then type in the passphrase to boot the OS. Truecrypt has this function as well.

As stated, it is not open-source. What that means is that it cannot be studied by the public sector (read: security users) to determine if any backdoors have been coded in. Like Truecrypt, it offers the option to create an encrypted operating system that holds a hidden operating system as well whose existence can be denied to those trying to harm or prosecute you. This is especially beneficial if you live in the UK, where failure to hand over a passphrase to an encrypted hard drive can get you two years in prison on a contempt of court charge. However you could give them the password to your decoy system. There is no way they could know if you were concealing a hidden operating system without a keylogger in place.

Truecrypt and Drivecrypt give no hints or leak any data regarding the existence of hidden files. The only way to mount said file is to know the password, and there are two you create with such an option: one for the decoy, and one for the hidden container/operating system.

Truecrypt and Drivecrypt also support the use of encrypted container files, which when clicked will mount the file the same way a mounting application like DaemonTools or Nero mounts an iso image. Prior to mounting, the application will ask you for the password. Mistype the password and the container does not mount at all. This can be very handy as there are a plethora of private items that you could conceal from government or any kind of prosecuting institution, such as medical records, tax records, school transcripts, business correspondence and the like.

Some tips for Truecrypt/Drivecrypt users:

1.) If you have one, disable the firewire port, as this can be used to reveal the encryption keys.

2.) Never leave any containers mounted on a laptop when crossing a border station, unless you want your private information in said container to be shared with the guards.

3.) Never leave your PC powered on and unattended for any lengthy amount of time (public wifi spots, cafes, libraries, college classrooms, etc). All security goes out the window when an attacker (or anyone else) has physical access to your machine. Neither Truecrypt nor Drivecrypt can protect your data in such a case, as the attacker can install a keylogger that can record your keystrokes.

Thumbnails: If you possess any incriminating snapshots (flings, Wikileak photos, informant docs) then at a later time delete the images in the folder, be aware that a shadow copy still exists. In windows XP (yes, legions of users are still clinging to this OS), thumbnails of jpegs are stored within each folder of the image's location. So if you have a folder called "government office snapshots", you will have thumbnails enabled in the folder settings tab for any pictures (jpegs, bitmaps, etc), and a hidden thumbs.db file will be present that shows a mini version of the picture in question. So even if you delete the jpegs, this hidden file will still reveal to anyone what the contents of the original folder were. The only way to see or disable this hidden file is to go to Tools – Options – View and set the option to "show hidden files and folders".

Until this is done, every single folder with pictures in it will store a mini-snapshot of the pictures unless this is disabled. Windows 7 is a completely different file system to Windows XP. Instead of keeping the thumbnail cache within the folder where the pictures reside, it stores it in a

central location
(`%userprofile%\AppData\Local\Micro soft\Windows\Explorer`)

I have found it much better to just leave the thumbnail option off in Windows 7, as the images load fairly quickly without the need for a cache to speed things up. There are other files, like text, audio and the like, that are also at risk of being discovered if you do not take precautions to securely delete the file. That does not mean deleted from the *recycle bin*, however. When you delete any items from the recycle bin, all that does is tell the operating system that the space previously occupied by that file can be written to again. It does not delete the file permanently until that space is overwritten to again by some other program.

Government agencies have programs that can *undelete* a file. The way around this is to use various programs to securely delete a file, such as Ccleaner. This app has an interesting wipe utility as well, in that it can wipe the free space of any previously deleted contents on the hard drive. You can even do this while the operating system is in use.

Needless to say, if you have a 2 terabyte hard drive and you're only using 20% of the drive, with 80% being "free space", then it will be a few hours for it to finish the wipe process, dependent on the speed of the hard drive and what other programs you have running. It does not touch any installed programs that exist already on the system unless you tell it to, and then only that free space that is allocated for use.

Swap file: Let's talk briefly about the "swap" file that most operating systems use. What this means is that sometimes during heavy PC usage, you will run low on system memory, and then the operating system will use your hard drive as a temporary ram storage device. This is what is called the "swap file", which increases the speed of computer operations. This swap file can be a veritable gold mine of data to someone with nefarious intentions. Text files, video thumbnails, and word document fragments can exist herein, enough to print out a pretty good snapshot of your past. There have even been court cases where people were convicted in court using nothing but thumbnail fragments. You can disable the swap file windows uses by going to control panel, System & Security, System, Advanced, Performance, Settings, Advanced, Virtual Memory and click Change. Choose "No Paging File". Reboot.

Note: Some resource intensive games use the swap file to speed up their games when there is not enough ram. If you run into any slowdowns with normal PC usage you can always switch this option back on, then reboot.

"There are two types of encryption: one that will prevent your sister from reading your diary and one that will prevent your government."

Bruce Schneier

Chapter 7 - I2P

I2P, otherwise known as the "Invisible Internet Project" is another option that people can use to hide their online IP address. It shares a lot of the same characteristics of other networks in that it routes traffic through neighboring peers. The developers have stated that their main goal is not necessarily one of 100% anonymity (a goal some say is impossible), but rather to make the system too troubling and expensive to attack from the outside. It is an *anonymizing* network with several layers of encryption wrapped around all the data that travels through the system.

I2P VS Tor

You might think this sounds a lot like Freenet, but the similarity is actually more like Tor's network. I2P offers interactivity with websites, blogs, forums, chat, search engines and all without the need to install any of them locally. Such are the hallmarks of I2P. Websites that exist in the I2P network are called Eepsites, and are hosted anonymously with I2P being a strict requirement to access these websites. In that vein, it is similar to the .onion sites accessible only via Tor. Every

PC that is connected to the I2P network shares in the forwarding of encrypted packets of data through proxies prior to the final destination. Each *subsequent* proxy prunes a layer of encryption at various intervals until encryption is removed. The bottom line is this: No one knows the origin of said packets, a trait also shared by Tor. While it is true that both Tor and I2P have different goals in mind, there exists many similarities:

- Both exist as anonymizing networks

- Both use layered encryption to funnel data

- Both have hidden services

- Tor has Exit Nodes and I2P has Outproxies

Benefits of Tor over I2P

- Larger user base than I2P; support from academic sources, constant improvements in stability and resistance to attacks
- Funding is sourced from many countries around the globe
- Large number of Exit Nodes
- Translated into many languages
- Optimized for Exit Traffic
- Memory more optimized than I2P
- Written in C

Benefits of I2P over Tor

- Hidden Services much faster than the Tor network.
- Not as many DOS (denial of service) attacks as Tor.
- Compatible with peer-to-peer file sharing (Tor is not).
- Tor tunnels last a long time compared to I2P. This ensures less attacks as the number of samples a hacker may use are limited.
- Every peer routes data for others.
- Offers TCP/UDP.
- Written in Java.

As you can see, both networks are safe enough for anonymity, as long as you aren't a world-hunted target. To this, a user's anonymity is typically broken due to their own sloppy behavior--their overconfidence being the weakest link in most cases (using the same login names on many websites, mixing these with Tor and non-Tor websites, and enabling JavaScript/Flash). Since I2P is not built to act as a proxy to the WWW, you should use Tor if you want to surf anonymously. The outproxies on I2P, as you've probably guessed, are similar to the exit nodes on Tor, but they do not have the greatest support and tend to be unstable. Thus you should use Tor for anonymous web browsing and I2P for I2p eepsites. One option is to use Foxy Proxy to test it yourself. Be aware however that since there are fewer outproxies than Tor exit nodes, it may be easier for an adversary to identify your activities. It all depends on how much risk you want to assume and what the ramifications are if you are caught (and in which country).

You can also use I2P for BitTorrent and iMule as well as other P2P applications. Like Freenet, you will find that I2P will grow in speed the longer you use it without interruption. Torrents will be faster. Data will come down like lightning. Tor users will thank you for it. There are already too many torrent users on Tor that clog the network and make it difficult for people in dire straits who need anonymity for their political actions far more than the next Incubus CD.

While I2P is a technical powerhouse for anonymity, it can be a bit like a house of cards. Once the Ace is pulled from the bottom layer (by you), it can be rendered moot. I2P is just a tool, as is Tor and Freenet. It is not an invisibility cloak. Do something stupid, like move too much when a pack of Orcs are looking your way, you're bound to get an arrow in a place where you least expect it. Thus, act smart by being proactive in anonymity:

1.) **Turn Off Javascript**

Yes, it bears repeating, with arms waving in the air and shouting at the top of our lungs. Javascript is the bane of not only Tor, but other networks that rely on cloaking your IP address. Leaving this beastly plugin ON allows code to be run on your

ıe, code that will decloak you. Look at your
ıer settings and disable it. Also disable
ıes. Super cookies are deployed in the wild to
ʿ down Tor users. Don't let it happen to you on
I2P. Javascript can reveal a ton of metrics that
fingerprint a user. Display resolution, page width,
font and so on can be sent to an adversary by
stealth. If you're in doubt, take a look at the web
API at Mozilla:

https://developer.mozilla.org/en-US/docs/Web/API

2.) **Silence is Golden!**

Don't say a peep. Sure, you can talk. But refrain
from discussing: the weather, your geography,
your hobbies, your city politician that was just
arrested for soliciting hookers. If someone says,
"Hows the weather in your town?" You say:
"Sunny." Every time. Alternatively, you may
misinform. The CIA does it, why can't you? Their
entire organization is built on secrecy and
deception. Don't get too choked up about a few
white lies. Spreading misinformation about trivial
things like the weather and the local politics can
really put a nail in an adversary's coffin. Ditto on
employment. If you are asked about your work and
you're a programmer, say you're a mail sorter
down at the Post Office. They're not going to ask
you about the latest Elvis stamp.

3.) **Rotate Usernames/Nics**

The desire for convenience often gets people in trouble. They use the same usernames on multiple sites/forums. That's fine for the daytime, open web. Not so much for the darknet. It breaks anonymity. Take forums for example. When your username becomes infamous for a wealth of knowledge, change it. Create a new one. Don't tell anyone. Entropy rises when many users swap information like this on a frequent basis. Maintain separate personas: one for the darknet, one for regular internet. Memorization is better than writing it down.

4.) **Never turn off your router**

I never turn mine off. Ever. If it is constantly going on and off while Freenet, Tor, I2P or IRC is running, after a while clues will surface as to who I really am, provided a sufficiently determined adversary has the resources to do it (NSA). The cost in power is negligible, so don't go cheap with anonymity. As the saying goes: out of speed, anonymity and reliability, you can only pick two, but make up for the lost component by acting *smart*.

5.) **Power in Numbers: Bandwidth**

Don't be stingy with your connection. The more you participate in the storm of users (Freenet, I2P), the more cloaked you will be. It is better to run 24/7 if you can. This makes it more difficult for an adversary to discern if you sent a file to someone else, or if you are merely the middle man to some file sent by a total unknown on the other side of the globe. Besides this, leaving the program running just makes it a lot faster network in general for other users. Think *Safety in Numbers*.

6.) **Optional (but smart)**

In the <u>browser settings</u>, set browser.safebrowsing.enabled and browser.safebrowsing.malware.enabled to false. Search goliaths like Google and Microsoft do not need to know the website URLs you visit.

Get into the habit of flushing the cache--cookies, etc. You can set this to do it automatically upon exit of the browser.

Refrain from using Foxy Proxy to selective proxy .i2p links. You don't want to be sent to the clearnet. If an I2P website is a honeypot, your Firefox browser can send a unique identifier in the referrer, in which case... anonymity broken.

At this point you're probably thinking this is way more headaches than it is worth. And you'd be right...in the beginning. But anything worth doing is usually hard at the outset. I as well as my colleagues do all of these things only because we have done them for years. We do them every day. Are we thinking about them? No, not in the least on account of smart habits done daily. Do you think intently about starting your car? Pulling out of the driveway? No. But it's a good bet you were petrified to do it when you were sixteen. And pulling out of your driveway is a very complex action, as are the aforementioned suggestions. Just one of your brain cells is more complex than a 747. Don't waste any of them.

Torrents and Eepsites

First things first. Install not only the NoScript plugin, but also the Cookie Whitelist (Buttons). Ideally you want to block everything when surfing Eepsites. There are a multitude of add-ons on the Firefox site but you do not need all of them. You only need the ones that preserve your anonymity.

Install QuickProxy, also at the Firefox site. Restart. Then open the proxy settings using the edit tab and then browse to "Preferences" and "Advanced". Then "Settings". Change your proxy settings to:

127.0.0.1 for HTTP Proxy, Port 4444 and 127.0.0.1 and port 4445 for SSL Proxy. Ensure Socks v4 is checked.

Click "Okay" and exit out. If you've configured it correctly you should be able to click the QuickProxy icon (lower corner of browser) when you browse Eepsites. You can also paste in .i2p websites and hit "Go" the old fashioned way.

Torrents

An option for torrents is to use I2PSnark. If you're a beginner, ensure the service is running by opening a terminal and inputing:

$ i2prouter status

If it is not running, start it with:

$ i2prouter status

Then browse via Firefox to

http://localhost:7657/i2psnark/

At the main I2PSnark page, you can see it running. Now you can create a torrent. Move a torrent and the data into

~/.i2p/i2psnark

The other option is to paste the data you want to seed to the same directory, and in my case, this is usually PDFs and technical manuals. At the Tracker option, you can choose whatever method you wish or create an entirely new torrent. I2PSnark will create the new torrent and set it in a queue. All that remains to be done is to click Start in the top corner and away you go.

Get your torrents from Postman's tracker:

http://tracker2.postman.i2p/

Torrents might be slow at first, but do not get discouraged. You will have far faster downloads on I2P than you ever will Tor. One can never have enough good karma in this world.

"I'm 16 now, I was 15 when it happened... and the encryption code wasn't in fact written by me, but written by the German member. There seems to be a bit of confusion about that part."

- Jon Johansen, Norwegian hacker who reverse engineered the DVD format

Chapter 8 - Facebook and Other Misfits

Facebook is a bit of a mixed bag where ethics is concerned. On the one hand, it is immensely popular and profit-inducing for a reason: people love to chat with relatives, old neighborhood friends, girlfriends, mistresses and political liaisons, all in real-time. People love connections. The feeling of unity and solidarity. The benefits are fairly immediate if you're the type of individual who likes instant gratification. There is nothing quite like the feeling of seeing old friends on your friend's list who you have not seen in twenty-five years, now instantly accessible for a chat session at just about any time of day.

It used to be that Facebook didn't rely as much on the IP address as a P2P network did. Times have changed. Nowadays, all of your personal information is theirs for the taking, and in some cases offered up on a digital platter by endusers. Your real name, phone number, who your past and present friends are, and even your pets are all valuable data as it can be targeted with advertising tailored to every atom of your personality. What could go wrong, you ask?

One problem facing Facebook users is that it is all too easy for Facebook to give this treasure trove of data up to the highest bidder. Worse, Facebook acts not as a protector of the 4th amendment, but as an destroyer of it. Many government agencies and local law enforcement have relied on Facebook profiles to establish alibis, reveal private emails, and prove or disprove acts that may be criminal or not. Read the Facebook privacy policy for yourself:

> "*We may also share information when we have a good faith belief it is necessary to prevent fraud or other illegal activity, to prevent imminent bodily harm, or to protect ourselves and you from people violating our Statement of Rights and Responsibilities. This may include sharing information with other companies, lawyers, courts or other government entities.*"

They're mandated by the government to abide by subpoenas for user information data except any private messages that are unopened and are less than 181 days of age (these require a warrant). The problem is that the Supreme Court never recognized a 4th amendment right to privacy. That is, data being shared with third parties, so the government pretty much has a blank check to engage in "shooting-fish-in-a-barrel" type expeditions for subscriber information that may or may not have anything to do with any criminal acts. State and corporation are thus conjoined at the hip in a quasi-fascism that is difficult to defeat and predict, nevermind the fact that the government often, when it has nothing else to do, creates laws that are meant to be broken--over and over (speed limits, anyone?).

Thus, outside of discussions on anonymity, there is a not much to do when the enemy's archers are standing upon the castle towers with flaming arrows aimed at the exposed king. But we'll try nevertheless.

Be mindful of what you type on Facebook. Actually, be paranoid, unless you are one of the king's fools. This should go without saying, but the neverending stream of fools on Facebook often don't even recognize your need for privacy or anonymity to say nothing of their own. They get so accustomed to the personalized interface that you start to think they've got in it for you with their shouting your real name across the internet. You are not anonymous here, or on any other social media site--Twitter, Pinterest, Google Plus, etc. In fact, a new Facebook account has even less privacy than one on a P2P network like Emule. Where emule is concerned, you only had to worry about the ip address. With Facebook, your private life belongs to them unless you take drastic action to prevent it. Yes, you may have heard more than a few complaints from a few peasants about the lack of privacy on Social Media. It hasn't failed to reached the ears of the ivory tower executives at Facebook, Inc. But what do they really think of anonymity?

The Anomaly: Anonymous Facebook Login

In April of 2014, CEO Mark Zuckerberg announced that Facebook planned to implement "Anonymous Login" for all users. It was a misnomer in the same way that "cat owner" is a misnomer. It offers more privacy, certainly, but not anonymity. It doesn't come close to anonymity since you cannot login to Facebook *anonymously*. What it means is that, using your Facebook login, you can sign in to other websites, say at Ars Technica or Wired, and make comments without having to grant access to the treasure of data Facebook holds on you: your list of contacts, relatives, friends, favorite cereals and the fact you hate cats with a brimstone passion.

Presently they are testing this so called "anonymity" service with a smattering of social sites and forums so as to better "benefit the end-user", as Zuckerberg claims--grant more control to its userbase on some of the data that gets transferred. Notice the word "some"... of the data. Not all.

And herein is the fallacy: most people, especially those on social media, do not know the difference between anonymity and privacy. Thus the masses will gobble it up. Certainly signing up for a new service can be cumbersome--email, check link, clink on link, fill out forms, click another link in email, fill out more forms. It's a breath of fresh air to know simpler times are in the pipeline, but let's call it what is: efficiency, not anonymity.

Most people will think Facebook will stand true to their anonymity statement, but the truth of it is that they lied to their userbase right out of the gate, trading the mundane term *privacy* for the much loftier goal of *anonymity*. Facebook knows all about these third party sites you visit, and is willing to offer the data up to the highest bidder. Your behavior, your identity, your favorites, all are a win-win for Facebook, and a lose-lose for the third party sites and *you*. If a nosy judge wants to uncloak you on a third party site over some "slanderous" comment you made, they need not go to the third party site. They will go to Facebook. They know the name you signed in with, the time you made the comment, the IP address you used to bounce to the discussion. Checkmate.

In an interview with Wired's Steve Levy, Zuckerberg had this to say about their new vision:

"When we were a smaller company, Facebook login was widely adopted, and the growth rate for it has been quite quick. But in order to get to the next level and become more ubiquitous, it needs to be trusted even more. We're a bigger company now and people have more questions. We need to give people more control over their information so that everyone feels comfortable using these products."

Sounds suspicious, does it not? Well, that's not to say it's good for the goose either. In this case, the third party. Website developers who decide to use Facebook's API to expand their readership will have that decision come back to haunt them since Facebook "controls" the client that uses the API login. They can shut off the API for the developers just as Nevada can shut off water piping out to California. To counter this, they will be ever more vigilant in mining user data and be hesitant, if not fully opposed, to using this new "anonymous" setting as it grants Facebook absolute rule over its userbase. That is, if they were *smart*. Many are not.

How to Be Anonymous on Facebook

Facebook is allergic to anonymity. You've probably heard that they frown on anonymous accounts. It is not entirely difficult to understand why. They can't target you with advertisements if they don't know who you are, and that's their bread and butter. From your behavior come the metrics, the things you buy, the places you enjoy visiting, your family links. From their own lips:

"We require everyone to provide their real names, so you always know who you're connecting with."

This is a roadblock that fortunately can be overcome, since genuine names are not yet tied to any form of government ID schemes like driver's licenses or social security numbers (though they will be someday). And even then, the rules of supply and demand would dictate even this would not dissuade the need for full anonymity.

When you are neck-deep in the account creation process at Facebook, you need to enter as much false data as you can. The email address in particular needs to be created in complete anonymity. The big mistake most people make is assuming that clocking the IP address is a sufficient means to the end. However there are many tracking mechanisms--complex algorithms designed to match behavior patterns and preferential choices--that all the big social media giants employ. Just one slip up, a broken link in the chain such as connecting to a website that knows your real identity (BBC, for instance) can destroy your every effort. Before you know it, all the others have been alerted by bots, warning pings and moderators that you've talked to in that session. Endgame.

Ask yourself this: Would your closest friends refer to you by name if you attended a popular masquerade in New Orleans during Mardi Gras? You bet they would, masked or not, even if you had pleaded with them to protect your identity. Some of them might whisper your name, not really even thinking about their prior oath of secrecy.

Then before you know it, another who happens to have the ears of a fox overhears your name being called. In much the same way, Facebook identifies you by your acquaintances just as others might do at the masquerade. Who is he talking to? A woman? Young or old? Tall or short? Do they talk with their hands? Ah, that's Maria from Rome. It's really not too difficult, and neither is it for Facebook. Friends and family lists are hardline identifiers in Facebook and Google's algorithms. The facial recognition Facebook employs can only get more advanced as it scours the web for matches elsewhere: Flickr. Google. Amazon. Twitter. Mugshot sites. Surveillance videos. Then there are photos of you to worry about: photos your friends have that are out of your control.

Facebook installs super cookies on your machine (or one of their many 3rd party enforcers) that tracks you in a number of ways: by Sid number, MAC address, etc. It continues to track you even after you've logged out of all your social media sites. There can be no such event as 100% anonymity just as there can be no such thing as a perfect human. We are the weak links.

But fear not, young Jedi. All is not yet lost.

While true anonymity is difficult, it is not impossible. We can approach 98% anonymity with some smart decisions. First things first. Invest in a VPN account. The more walls we have between us and the target, the stronger the cloak. Visibility is cloudy in a VPN as they shield many of your moves. Location awareness is difficult to detect using a VPN, but avoid free public proxies as Facebook and every other site has been spammed to death with them and have shielded themselves from those range of IP addresses. Thus, a proper (well-respected) VPN is the way to go. You will want speed to blend in with other non-anonymous users. Every metric counts.

You will need to disable most cookies from third-parties but allow Facebook for each session. Using Firefox portable, you can set the browser to auto-clear them upon exiting each session.

Set up your false data. Everything must be different from anything you've set at any other forum. Ars Technica, Wired, WSJ--they're all in bed with Facebook to one degree or another. Ensure complete uniqueness, and under no circumstances give them your mobile phone number, as this will nuke your anonymity before it gets off the ground. That number, along with the IP, is used primarily for targeted advertising as well as by law enforcement. You may have noticed that Yahoo now requires it for new accounts. The reason is that it makes things easier to identify you.

Avoid a large group of friends and NO RELATIVES. This can't be stressed enough. Relatives, especially the elderly, love to gossip and spill details about the retched veal you cooked last night, or the cat you sprayed with the garden hose last week. What you don't hear in other's chat boxes at Facebook can harm you. Politely tell (never ask) others not to tag you or refer to any events that may compromise you: pictures, videos, music that your "real self" enjoys. Three breadcrumbs is enough to raise the eyebrow of the algorithm. Insist on them calling you by a nickname. If they refuse, remove them.

Never use the same browser for your VPN that you use for non-VPN sessions. Install Firefox portable in its own directory with its own shortcut and configured to the VPN BEFORE creating the Facebook account. Never mix them up. You don't want cross-cookie contamination.

Be cautious on other social sites as well: Google, Twitter, Pinterest, MySpace. Facebook will not invest in the resources to find you unless you hand them crumbs of data yourself, which can easily be done on other sites you are careless with. So avoid being too specific about things related to your hardwired beliefs on those other sites, too: Religion. Politics. Ethics. Switch them up. Be a Buddhist for a session or two. Or a non-practicing non-denominationalist. Just be mindful of stirring up a hornet's nest. A friend in Thailand (an American) who was well known in Freenet insulted the Thai king on Facebook, prompting them to take a magnifying glass to his account. The end result? Facebook changed his name without his authorization--to reflect his *real identity*. Embarrassing. He'd posted a link to his page on Freenet as well and as you can imagine, his entire identity was uncovered by this loud behavior.

It is not possible to convert your existing Facebook profile into an anonymous one no matter how many tweaks you make. Changing the name will do nothing. The algorithm (think of the sentinels from The Matrix) will still have records of your online behavior as well as your IP address. Privacy, however, *is* obtainable, in case you wish to shield your identity from nosy coworkers or other misfits. In this case you need to change your username, that part of the profile others see then tweak the privacy settings accordingly with how invisible you wish to be. It is a bit of a double-edged sword since this will make it harder for others to see you--those you may *wish* to see you. You'll have to seek them out yourself and add them. And this, too, can reveal your true identity. Nothing typed into Facebook is ever truly invisible from the bots at their disposal.

"These days. Most of us have the attention span of a meth-addicted squirrel."

- Kristen Lamb, Rise of the Machines

Chapter 9: Tails

Edward Snowden. The name rings a bell for most people around the globe. In tech circles he is a visionary. As for the non-techies, a few labels come to mind: Whistleblower. Hero. Traitor. Regardless of what you pin him with, one thing is certain: He hates censorship and loves anonymity, the kind of anonymity that calls for untrackable execution. Before discussing anything, he insisted liaisons use not only PGP (pretty good privacy) but the end-all-be-all of anonymity tools: Tails-- a thief-simple tool that frustrates even those in the upper echelon of the NSA. And for good reason, since even they do not know the wizard who designed it.

Where Tor is the worm of the anonymous fisherman, Tails is the fishing box. The fish at the other end have no idea who is inside the boat, watching, listening. It's a hacker's tool but also a patriot weapon. Using it is a breeze: install it on a USB stick, CD, whatever, boot from said stick and find yourself cloaked and shielded from the NSA, provided that you don't out yourself. And if you're using Tails, you're smarter than that anyway.

Built upon the shell of Linux, it acts as an operating system and comes with an assortment of nukes to launch under Big Brother's nose: Tor browser, chat client, email, office suite and image/sound editor, among others.

Snowden preferred Tails on account of its no-write rule: no direct data writing. A breach from a remote adversary? Not going to happen. Forensics investigation? Nope. No trace is going to be left on the DVD/USB. Obviously this is a no brainer to use if you're an NSA employee looking to spill the beans on unconstitutional spying, as well as a must-have for political dissidents and journalists. It is armored with plausible deniability, the same as Truecrypt.

Tor runs like warm butter when you boot with Tails. There's not much of a learning curve, and no excessive tweaking required. You can use it in the same PC you use at work. Boot from USB or DVD. Do your thing then reboot back into your normal PC with no record or footprint of your Tailing. For all intents, you're a ghost on the internet. And speaking of ghosts, the creators of Tails are anonymous themselves. No one knows their identities. But what we do know is that they will not bow to governments trying to muscle a backdoor into the code.

Linus Torvalds, creator of Linux, said in 2013, "The NSA has been pressuring free software projects and developers in various ways," implying that they had made the effort, and all with taxpayer funds. A bit like the cat saying to the mouse, "Transparency is good for you. Sleep out in the open and not the damp and dark, flea-infested mousehole." They don't like secrets.

You might be asking, how do we *know* that Tails does not already *have* a backdoor? How do we know that the NSA has not already greased their hands? The evidence is twofold: the code is open-source (anyone can audit it), and the mere fact that the NSA made an effort to sideline end-users says they fear such a powerful package. They cannot peer inside to see what the mice are doing. Snowden claimed that the NSA, while he was with them, was a major thorn in the side of that organization.

At the time of Tails conception five years ago, the interest had already started to build up in the Tor community for a more cohesive toolbox. "At that time some of us were already Tor enthusiasts and had been involved in free software communities for years," they said. "But we felt that something was missing to the panorama: a toolbox that would bring all the essential privacy enhancing technologies together and made them ready to use and accessible to a larger public."

PGP is also included in package. You owe it to yourself and peace of mind to learn it. Spend a Sunday with it and you'll be a competent user. Spend a week and you'll be an enthusiast. As well, KeePassX can be useful if you want to store different info (usernames, pass phrases, sites, comments) into one database. These two are like a good set of gauntlets no aspiring black knight would do without. And don't think the blacksmiths have just smelted down some cheap metal, either.

The designers have gone to a lot of trouble to modify the privacy and security settings. The more they do, the less you have to.

This is not to say you should use Tails every day. Only use it in those times you feel anonymity is warranted. As mentioned before, if you start mixing up services, operating systems and mac addresses, you may blow your cover. Though Tails is packaged with programs that one wouldn't normally associate with anonymity (GIMP, OpenOffice, Audacity, etc) you don't want to leak info where an adversary might build a profile on you. You'd be shocked at how many applications these days "dial home" without your knowledge (hint: almost all of them).

But the true Achilles heel is the *metadata.* Tails is really lousy at hiding it. It doesn't try to. It doesn't clear any of it nor does it encrypt the headers of your encrypted emails. Are you an ebook author? Be careful about PDFs and .mobi files, as depending on which software you use, it can store the author's name and creation date of your work. But this is not really the fault of Tails. Rather, it is the wishes of the development team to stay compatible with the SMTP protocol.

The other problem with metadata is pictures: JPEGs, TIFF, BITMAPS and so on, which again, depending on the software, can store EXIF data-- data that stores the date the picture was taken as well as the GPS coordinates of the image. Newer cameras and mobile phones like Samsung Galaxy are notorious for this, and even keep a thumbnail of the EXIF data intact for nose parkers with nothing to do all day but to sniff through other people's property. A fake GPS spoofer may be useful but even that won't eliminate the exif data. You'll need a separate app for this. You might even go so far as to only use formats that don't store any metadata at all. Plain-text is one option, though even that can be watermarked.

You might think, "Can I hide Tails activity?" The short answer is: maybe. It depends on the resources of the adversary. And just who is the adversary? The government? The private detective? The employer? The fingerprint Tails leaves is far less visible than what Tor leaves. And yes, it is possible for an administrator to see you are using Tor, as well as your ISP. They cannot tell what you're doing on Tor, mind you, but there are Tor Browser Bundle users, and Tails users. It all comes down to the sites you visit.

We've seen how they can build a profile on you from your resolution, window metrics, addons and extensions and time zones and fonts, but to alleviate this the Tails developers have tried to make everyone look the same, as if they were all wearing white Stormtrooper armor. Some fall through the cracks, making themselves easier for a correlation attack by installing too many addons and thus marking themselves in the herd: A purple-colored stormtrooper, if you will. Such and such user has a nice font enhancer while no other user does. This alone does not break anonymity, but with a hundred other factors and sufficient resources, it might be the one detail that breaks the house of cards. Death by a thousand stings.

You might find Tor bridges (alternative entry points on Tor) to be a good investment in reading, as they can better hide you from your ISP. In fact, using a bridge makes it considerably harder for your ISP to even know you are using Tor. If you decide this route (and you should if merely using Tor can get you arrested-- a case in which you should NOT use the default Tor configuration), the bridge address must be known.

Be mindful of the fact that a few bridges can be obtained on the Tor website. If you know about it, others do too--even adversaries like the NSA, but it is still stronger for anonymity purposes than the default Tor config. Like Freenet, it would be optimal if you personally know someone in a country outside the USA who runs a private obfuscated bridge that has the option *PublishServerDescriptor 0*. As always, luck favors the prepared.

"The government does things like insisting that all encryption programs should have a back door. But surely no one is stupid enough to think the terrorists are going to use encryption systems with a back door. The

terrorists will simply hire a programmer to come up with a secure encryption scheme."
  Kevin Mitnick

Chapter 10: How to Defeat the NSA: a Guide to Staying Anonymous

It needs to be said. The time is nigh for the NSA to dissolve. If not dissolved, then at least broken up as Nazi Germany was after WWII. Mission creep, the expansion of a project beyond its original goals (often after initial successes) has reared its ugly head once again as the NSA, once known as "No Such Agency", has far surpassed its original purpose: to secure American communications while gathering intel on our enemies. Unfortunately, it seems *we* have become the enemy. We, the path of least resistance, so to speak.

Intelligence gathering is now such a high priority to the NSA that it has gone global at the expense of sovereign security. The Tailored Access Operations (TAO) directive makes this obvious. Install spyware/backdoors on the enemy's computers... well and good until Snowden revealed that they do the same to their own countrymen. It's called *bulk surveillance*. The more data they have, the louder they are on claiming victory over the usual boogeymen: Terrorists. Drug lords. (how long was it to catch Bin Laden?). Emails, calls, even video is collected without your consent. You could say it is a system ripe for abuse, if it were not already rotting from the inside out due to the Patriot Act (section 215). The very notion that the

NSA can shield itself from Congress and the taxpayers who foot the bill should appall most Americans.

So, what to do when the mother eagle turns on her chicks? Answer: Build your own nest. First things first, however. Understand that if you are a high value target like Bin Laden or a Mafia don, the NSA will hack your internet-connected computer or phone regardless. There's no getting around it. If you're thinking, "Well, I paid a hundred clams for Drivecrypt and Phonecrypt and so it is safe from those hucksters," there is some bad news for you to swallow, cowboy. It is far from safe.

Drivecrypt is commercial software and closed-source, and considering the free offerings out there (Truecrypt--open-source and *audited*), the best case would be that you're only paying for the name. Worst case? The NSA has a backdoor within the code, or at least knows of an exploit no one else knows about. You can thank the NSA's BULLRUN program, which attempts to "insert vulnerabilities into commercial encryption systems, IT systems, networks and endpoint communication devices."

In an ideal, pro-Constitution country, the security of the citizenry against foreign threats would be priority one. Instead, we are faced with a well-funded behemoth that considers the monitoring and data farming of *citizens* priority one. Again, think "least resistance". Hacked accounts from Blizzard to Kickstarter to Yahoo occur every month and the NSA seems helpless to stop it. Only the truth is a little different than they led us to believe.

They do have the means to stop it, as it turns out. But it would require a significant rerouting of resources so that citizens are protected and not monitored and assumed guilty of some obscure crime. Worse, the positions of authority and influence are unbalanced and skewed. Cyber Command should not be integrated with NSA priorities at all. Their priorities should be focused abroad, *like all other military operations*, and not focused on citizens like some Eye of Sauron that creates crime out of thin air.

Luckily, a few have leaked enough data from the NSA's coffers to mount a counteroffensive. One man cannot undo the damage they've done, but a nation can: the millions can overpower their overreach and send them back to their proper place.

How?

Knowledge is power. This hardly changes over time and for the NSA, the knowledge resides in the network itself. That's where the NSA loves to probe and plant their bugs. To this, they farm all the data. Everything. Then hire analysts to sort it all. They monitor phone calls, satellite messages and even listen to the oceanic cables running to and fro to our allies. They tap the waterfall at the source, high above, or beneath our feet if need be. Good intel, ripe for the sifting.

But what is good intel to them? Well, it's whatever sets off the most flags: the people involved, their countries, the language they use, their religion. It all gets prioritized based on profiles their algo agents categorize. The more red flags, the higher up the totem pole it goes... into a wellspring of *metadata*. It is easier to cherry pick targets by examining metadata than to study complete emails and conversations. It saves time. It saves money. Metadata to the NSA is like cocaine to a drug dealer. It's valuable stuff.

The Systems Intelligence Directorate does the data sifting and sorting in this case, and is given billions by Congress to optimize its operations every year. They are always updating and honing their capabilities. Testing what works and what doesn't. A security group exists for each directive handed down by the brass. They do nothing but look for ways to streamline each infiltration tactic. Make it all blood simple with the push of a button, a button that has global outreach.

NSA agents can infiltrate at will, but they especially love non-updated hardware like routers. When was the last time you updated your router encryption key? Right. The NSA knows this as well. They have a backdoor for many of them and entire teams devoted 24/7 to finding exploits for every brand of router and password encryption scheme. This is all accomplished by the TAO

red Access Operations). Once inside your
they can easily install a custom-made
/logger that records your keystrokes and will
nd them quietly under the radar. Your anti-virus
will not detect it. Once this is done, it doesn't
matter how complex your password is. Thus, it is
easy to see how valuable prevention is.

But how does one prevent such an intrusion
from a well-funded entity? The answer is
encryption. Encrypt your email. Your data. Your
boot pass phrase. Most people will not bother with
email. Some might bother with data. And fewer
still will bother with encrypting the entire OS as it
can take hours for a 2TB hard drive.

A few strict security suggestions:

I) The NSA does not like Tor. It's expensive to
track users. When a lot of money is asked of
Congress, they start asking questions and
demanding results. They don't want *anyone* asking
questions. So use Tor. However, do not say
anything in an email that you would not recover
from if it was broadcasted on network TV. And do
not access your normal email account or bank
account using Tor. Can you see why?

II.) Invest in an offline netbook or laptop for
mission critical data. Make encrypted backups:
Blu-Ray, USB, SD. Never allow the data onto your
internet PC unless in encrypted form: Truecrypt

containers/PGP encrypted, etc. Only decrypt messages offline and away from the internet. Learn about SSL/IPsec. Many Usenet providers offer SSL for free but leave it off by default. Turn it on.

III.) Whenever possible, avoid commercial encryption packages. The proprietary software is almost never audited, unlike Truecrypt. What does that tell you when they are afraid of people looking at their code? They're hiding something from you. When an encryption program is open-source, it is more secure, not less, because others can verify its security and detect any back doors. Word spreads like wildfire when a backdoor is discovered, but not if the door is nailed shut from the other side.

IV.) Your screen lock does not have to be perfect. It won't keep out any government agents but it may keep out nosy wives and friends. If however the OS is not encrypted and your laptop is stolen, all your data is theirs for the taking. Use an open-source app like Password Safe to secure them all from prying eyes.

You're probably thinking, why do you need all of these tools for privacy? Shouldn't Truecrypt or SSL for your Usenet be enough? The short answer is: it depends. It depends on your own level of risk. What you can live with if all is lost. And your loss is the NSA's gain, through threats of lawsuits and coercions and unconstitutional spying. They've almost succeeded in turning the web into a vast Orwellian looking glass-- with themselves as the only keymasters. They can only succeed if good men do nothing.

Trust encryption like you trust ammunition. And like ammunition, it can be learned in a weekend. Mastery however takes some time and effort, but know that by itself, it will do nothing but allow tyranny to flourish unless used for its original purpose.

Endgame

Hopefully if you have read this far, then you are now aware of some of the dangers that await us in the future. Clearly, having an exposed IP address is only a drop in the ocean next to the coming power grab. Unfortunately, there are always going to be up and coming social networks and applications that try to go above and beyond the use of the IP address to monitor you. We have seen it happen with many personal applications over the years: Internet Explorer, Napster, Limewire, Myspace, Facebook and the like. These make their profits by subverting your personal choices and then targeting you based on those choices, and when you get right down to it, the longer you put off protecting your individuality, the less choice you will have in the long run. However, you now have at least an effective arsenal of tools in which to minimize this subversion. If enough people take notice, it may stem or even reverse the tide of fascism coming over the hills.

More and more we are seeing a gradual erosion of privacy. Some employers reject applicants to entry level positions based on credit score. Some employers demand Facebook usernames and passwords before hire. Some fire employees for words on a Facebook post. In the end it is all about control and eroding individual choice. For there is no one in the universe more unique than you. You are worth more than all the stars combined, and they know it. And want to control it. And there is no such thing as controlling just a little bit of a star.

Stay safe, always.

Made in the USA
San Bernardino, CA
18 April 2019